D1360480

Poems by Michael Coffey

87 NORTH

COFFEE HOUSE PRESS MINNESOTA

PS
3553
.0362
A615
1999

Coffee House Press is supported in part by a grant provided by the
Minnesota State Arts Board, through an appropriation by the
Minnesota State Legislature, and in part by a grant from the National
Endowment for the Arts. Significant support has also been provided
by the McKnight Foundation; the Lila Wallace Reader's Digest Fund;
Lannan Foundation; Target Stores, Dayton's, and Mervyn's by the
Dayton Hudson Foundation; General Mills Foundation; Jerome
Foundation; St. Paul Companies; Butler Family Foundation;
Honeywell Foundation; Star Tribune Foundation; James R. Thorpe
Foundation; the law firm of Schwegman, Lundberg, Woessner &
Kluth, P.A.; and many individual donors. To you and our many readers
across the country, we send our thanks for your continuing support.

Coffee House Press books are available to the trade through our
primary distributor, Consortium Book Sales & Distribution, 1045
Westgate Drive, Saint Paul, MN 55114. For personal orders, catalogs,
or other information, write to: Coffee House Press, 27 North Fourth
Street, Suite 400, Minneapolis, MN 55401. Good books are brewing
at www.coffeehousepress.org.

LIBRARY OF CONGRESS CIP INFORMATION
Coffey, Michael, 1954 –
      87 north : poems / by Michael Coffey.
            p.   cm.
      ISBN 1-56689-085-3 (ALK. PAPER)
      I. Title. II. Title: Eighty-seven north.
PS3553.0362A615   1998
811'.54—dc21   98-56290
                                                                    CIP

10   9   8   7   6   5   4   3   2   1
first printing / first edition
printed in Canada

40588325

Contents

Part One

Part Two

Part Three

Part Four

"Meaning is the dialect we speak at home."

—Jean Day, *The Literal World*

PART ONE

In Robert Motherwell's Car

Above a cliff
a boy could see it—
the dented funnel
atop Doyle's farmhouse

spewing smoke. Go on ahead,
Dad says, so up the flags
I stamp, flags tamped into the turf
a hundred years ago. Dad coughs and hacks.

❋

What's nine-and-a-half hours
from where the Shinnecock squat
over shallows
to the rocky outcrops of the Mohawk?

❋

Truths, like aphorisms, are a line long.

I never saw
what Dad said fell
off the mountain that night.
Some gazelle or a weasel

jumped, maybe a lynx; just sprang
from the spring above the road
and roared, white in the moonlight. "Jaun-
diced eyes," Dante said, or maybe Doyle did.

❋

Perfectly to live, to live life
perfectly, is to be filled with rage
at a world fallen and rife—
that's right—with assholes.

❋

Nah, to have a few thoughts is all.

"Like all revolutions, it substituted some
new restrictions for old ones. . . . Real freedom would be
to use this method when it could be
of service and correct it. . . . Sexual liberty,

[Breton] proclaimed, meant every conceivable
sexual act
except for homosexuality
[René Crevel, René Crevel, René Crevel]," wrote Ashbery.

❀

The unsightly genetic collision
of a LaDue and a DeFayette, once wed,
yields a humpbacked, slant-eyed,
fish-mouthed being, an *echt*-marlin.

❀

Rigmarole and upstate towns.

Made of birchbark and wicker,
was prodded along in the surf by a stick,
kind of a catamaran
that carried a baby Indian.

A mother, shin-deep, moved with it, just off shore,
starting somewhere near Sagaponack
heading west the length of Long Island . . .
. . . ahead to New York Bay . . .

❉

. . . up the Hudson to Lake Champlain
and along the St. Lawrence northeast
to the wide, briny Atlantic, a dream . . .
. . . down the coast to Boston and ashore.

❉

From Ausable, Rockwell Kent lit out for Greenland.

Evening, we were visiting.
I am Eddie, my father's boy
but 10 years old,
a part of the evening, like the flies

and the Fleischmann's whiskey
and the flyer for the county fair,
fawned over, I was, was me,
by Dad and Doyle and Dante.

❋

. . . Hutchinson to the Cross County Expressway,
then you hit 87 North.
Take that for all it's worth
straight home.

❋

Headlights swing down Steve Ryan's hill, freeze you in your chair.

Knowing like I know now
you learn to make exceptions
and change—a kind of allowance
for chance and natural disorder.

I stay sober these days, half-
way there, kind of like an alphabet
you tire of after M or so, the music stops.
Suddenly, is old, is deaf.

※

It is our forms that fail us,
with some purpose. At the sixty-foot pool
above the stretch of river now forbidden to swim
I go with my kids, see a family of DeLormes.

※

The shape of desire never changes.

Doyle or yellow lilies evolve—
Dali after Long Island
made a Tristan Tzara arras
even René [Crevel] never said took.

Still, I'm Jack L'Aventreur, in a bistro
in a Breton piece I saw
at Guild Hall in Easthampton.
I am Donati's spooky decalcomanias . . .

    ❋

. . . and Maya Deren's *At Land,* shot
at Amagansett on the beaches, sand
in black and white, shells, a dead man,
a chess piece, oh me.

    ❋

Ernst's *King Playing with His Queen* in Robert Motherwell's car.

Late one night I stop
at our Redford Church and go in.
The tan and ochre fieldstone
house of worship where I spent

Sunday mornings. Mom, Dad: we sat in the same pew.
It's dark now. Who cares? Churches are open
all hours in the country.
I have a lot of drink in me.

✻

My friend says it's spin control, dude.
He knew Dad, was a nephew to Doyle.
Randy's one man who's seen the face of God.
He lost an eye to it.

✻

There's the thing in the trees, and the wind.

I walk slowly—*thunk*—into glass doors: these are new,
the vestibule leading to the aisle.
Recovering, I walk down the nave, furtively,
feigning guile

to the communion rail. I can't see the statues
along the sides—who'd want to?
I kneel and make the sign of the cross.
And for a moment look at Jesus.

❉

And I know him, and through him
he knows me. The Son says I'm fucking up.
What's new? I say He is, too.
We have an arrangement.

❉

Ermine is a weasel, pal.

Thus Doyle (or Dali) after Dad died
(not Dante) telling me, all dewy-eyed,
what's what, in a voice like tar.
A shock: he knew the poets of the Great War.

Who would have known it?
Sure, with the D&H
he'd been to every county in the state,
including Yates and Wyoming. But Wilfred Owen?

❊

Shoulders of a marlin. Head of a pin.
It could move an engine block
with one hand (or fin?)
and count to ten.

❊

A dull cruelty; a remembered infidelity cools me.

And if it's alabaster I wouldn't know it.
It's pink, dusty, chipped
like old cake frosting, plaster
maybe, the body of Christ, his robe.

In the car still running
warm in the winter
I have the radio on.
Some song I know, some rocker.

❋

I say, "C'mon, take me, sucker.
You took the railroad guy Dad knew named Doyle."
Ha. He's like me:
he won't listen.

❋

In the world and out of it, stay on its roads.

God. They never spoke of him (or her?)
but of Rockefeller, yessir. Whence this sense
of cement I've had ever since
to the town "Gouverneur." Oh roads . . .

How what was built was built. And why.
Seein' how the cards are played,
said Doyle, and seein' 'em right.
Dad nods through the smoke like he has it made.

＊

I'll tell you: it's 500 miles
Montauk to Saranac, exit 37
off the Northway; a short while
west on Route 3, you're there.

＊

Wet hay in the barn, burning.

Of Doyle what remains of his house—
I drive by—
are the staggered flags going up the hill.
Dante's dead, I've said. So's Dad. The knoll flat

where the house used to pitch
as I drive by
and still don't know
what lasts of what's written.

By Whale Light

I fancy I suppose a poem
made of poem's lights,
a wall made of cement
where poured letters harden.

Fancy a sentence fenced
with straight slats of wood
rather than words, a life
lived of lifetimes, not moments.

Life of a piece, alphabets
but objects you rearrange
like Lisa said, as symbols
of themselves, jarsful of jars,
trucks towing tow trucks,

abecedaries, a chocolate
eatery, want never wanting;
the finger in the skin of a glove,
love, something complete

as a perfect vocable, the far-
flung, the gullible, the sea
made of sea sights, the sky
just what sky is.

I see Stubb, was it, second mate,
eating whale by its own light.
Good Ishmael judged it sin?
Man, dig the knife in.

The Wind

Not kites, the wind didn't loft us
like some magical lift does, as kids
we didn't do kites in the spring
we fished.

It blew, more than that, the wind howled
in the evenings or just at dawn
and pulled us or scared us
from beds or back into cars,

metal bunged by its blows
and rattling; even the covers fled.
The wind soared as a thing that read
other things like fingers braille—

the wheat, the trees, the barn door
waving as, wending as, wind does,
leaving a speech across the grass
that the day could see and the crows.

Melville on the Beach

Pounding, again, assurances of the surf,
a ceaseless splash of water worrying
black rocks back to depths and down . . .

The heaving, sloshing lots
of urgencies renewed, ocean's
renewal, storm-heightened
by small squalls of protest mustered
at the world's stoniness, the brass . . .

And then a relenting, an easeful
backing to a steadier state,
rhythm's assertion
that all is plain in water and air,
and the sea is full of syllables.

Trees of Knowledge

It's all about the trees, then—
bare, budding, in bloom,
there they are.

Older than the people
who walk beneath them,
or destined to be

taller, deeper, more broad.
And out there all night.
When the birds sleep, or not,

when the sky opens
or winks,
we don't know what trees do

or would. God is there,
if God there is, draping
His hair down

into the rigid branches
for a scratch.
They laugh,

since God knows
that trees know
Man has been forgiven

for all his sins.
That was the plan:
His Son died

on a tree
but we don't get it.
Their laughter is silent

and long with joy.
We are free
but don't condone it.

This is the knowledge,
Look!
It's all about the trees now.

But No

So it's about learning things, then,
and knowledge,
or are we fooled
by synchrony

when odd rhymes
chime like happenstance
among the living
and what we remember of the dead?

What I know best is probably chewing
and no one taught me that:
the what, the when, the how.
Is this what saved me, or what I should be saved from?

"From" is the limp word here, not "image."
It connects things to things
and people to people.
Hume wrote his history of England

backwards, distrustful of *from.*

The mouth is of itself, where we chew.
All else issues there, the spew
of words and whistles and spittle,
clucks of love and leavings,

sallies of ideas tongue-twisted
into tales of what we know
or want, or what we thought we heard
on the mount

delivered as choppings in air
to someone's ear, stories
about the fathers and the boys
and the women, every damn noise, all

amplified from the gut
where lives live like coils around a pole,
a charge of thought and sound
that can be etched a million ways,

one of them being poetry.

III.

What *do* I know?
is the question to ask.
And I wish I had an answer
or an idea

that somehow would find an image,
like water in a glass
and where it came from
and how the glass itself

is somehow the mind.
Like Stevens's "light
is a lion that comes down to drink,"
imagination as some wild predator,

proud, powerful, silent,
padding with a thousand pounds of stealth
across the veldt,
its tongue ready

to break a pane of sky.

At Sagaponack

There are rhythms to life and language—
the sea, the moon, the blood.
You know them well.
                              Without them
you can't play pool or fuck,

know when to cleanse a wound,
or play the long shot,
say when enough is enough
and it's time to go home.

So truth is to be dealt with—
There is a rhythm to things . . .
if you can find it.
                              If you
stand at the seaside, squint
into the breeze, hear the shore

lap and lap, the sush-slap
and laughter of silly waves
                              breaking over, free
and effortlessly, and forever

they tang with salt
                    the tongue
and make eyebrows bead
in the spray, the wind bells
around the ear, hollowing voices
inside which sound can sit
and clear . . .
                    Then you can
hear perhaps a lovely music
coming off the water, gathering
such slight feints and tones
      of silence and noise
as to be a language
                    you recognize,
the words it has gathered
                         are yours,
you know them,
                    the language of the sea,
today, telling you as it has always done,

that on any day and for many years
men will listen to the sound
                         of anything, thinking
this is thinking.

First Snow

Fresh snow, first snow,
known to all men—
the coming of the winter
and the cold.

First snows of December,
all praise Him—
pointless and divine,

this falling, His falling down
in numbers of flakes
impossible to know.

Fresh snow, touch my tongue,
white and irresolute—
I mean without resolve, Lord—
let the snow come down hard.

PART TWO

Rhythm City

Winter salt stains white on the sidewalk
chalked like a frost in the cement,
shadow patterns of a cold frigid nonsense
underfoot. Frozen spit there like a nickel,

gray and round and chunked to the pavement—
someone's saliva not long ago, now cooled,
bacterium caught mid-swim in enzymes
spat into the cold stilled world like an oath.

Rough kinds of roads, the shapes of ideas.
A roomful of brass bars off West Broadway—
Walter De Maria. Thuds, studies of thuds
impact upon the culture like a tooth gone bad
and must be fixed. So it gets fixed.

Windblown, insistence, the beat
of in and out, of air
through a doorway
or a blind, the thucking,
soft rattle of a window
frame, warped. A rattle chatter.

Life and death between portals
full of breath, the house
an absence outside
that's endlessly breathing in

its insistence, I suppose,
on what you cannot stop
doing, even in sleep.

For some reason
I find these thirteens.
Poems just that long, lines . . .
three stanzas most are. Even this

talking-about-sleep
one, where subject and object
collapse, like before, the sleeper asleep
and no word from the spoken.

Now that it's clear
I wonder about this lack: a missing line,
an orphaning like a missing breast. I wonder
about my ones: eleven eleven I was born.
That's one one one one.

It's natural, I guess,
the measurable length of a thought,
how long it takes to launch
this thought, or to beach it,

entangling with
what I know, as it will, lingering
there, finding, moving on
toward what I need to
before getting out.

Reluctant to overstay
a welcome, knowing how
welcomes always come first
and the first forgotten.

One line short
of a sonnet, okay: Have I
always thought sonnets
one line too long? Victims

of a sad rhyme scheme, love of
pairs, inability to
abandon one to ones?
Which is odd, really,

when that which cannot stand
so well, unbalanced
on a very spindly leg,
falls from a world forever free,
and on and on, about language.

And reflections on being—
that swallowed-exalted-everything-whole
that fills the days
with a kind of promise
held, as held is held—in truth
a kind of feeling.

One wants it to be so.
Not a life of work or life of play
but of memories—love being
loved, old love
being conscious, stayed,

resident in expression, no:
the idea of expression.

Enormous lozenges.
Why do they comfort me so?
Things large and to be swallowed
again, and swallowed black.

I mean habitual invocations
of a senseless, brutish beast
like a musician might conjure,
blowing the same round squawk.

It does crouch there.
It is a beast.
Fats Waller's heavy breathing
you can hear over the keys
all that rhythm, all that flesh.

Rhythming, what was it?
Monk's thing:
"Rhythm-a-ning," at the Five Spot.
1958. Roy Haynes on drums,
Johnny Griffin on tenor sax,
Ahmed Abdul-Malik
on bass, nineteen
and fifty-eight.

No hepcat shit. No more.
Baldwin called Brando
a beautiful cat, then, when.

Monk on piano.
That's that.

Consuming like a fire
all the bramble you breathe in,
even this, this voice
tossed to the sordid heat
crackles the cool night air.

The wind whips it down,
flames like the hair on a boy
jumping in a downdraft.
But the eyes are wild
with amazement.

How can this be?
No one's going to die,
the boy seems to want to say.

A flight of exalted birds,
an ear that flames,
the thin mid-distance gaze
of a man swallowing

his sick on the sidewalk,
wet brown string
or someone's guts
glazing in the sunlight
of uncertain baked goods
arguing an earnest point
to a teller machine.

It is this, he admits, looking down:
Can't dance.

St. Vincent's

A smell in the air
this morning
of lime and peppermint.
I stick my nose in it,
into the wind,
and shut my eyes.

A skein of cloth
or a streamer flapping,
loving its own furlings.
I think perhaps
it is ammonia now
laid over
a scent of citrus.

The smell from long ago,
a medicinal smell
here before the hospital
in which I was born,
in the early morning,
doors wide open to the air.

Mid-life, Looking North

Tendering motes in falls of light
siftingly, like soft flakes of soap,
drift in a column of space
over Fifth Avenue.

The steady solid forms of the street—
architectures deeply footed, high, broad-
shouldered stones faced in gallant glass:
mixture of air and lives.

Stood on pavement, one eye in a slow storm,
a motion tracing what is life, a pastime;
the persistent erasing is it
of disarticulated spaces, other's spices?

A long Wednesday, anyway, getting longer.
Struck like Yeats in a London shop,
not with blessing or the blessed, but torso-stocked,
iron-lunged, a soul turning into things.

John Cheever

Just telling is how it was for him, always telling. He'd just
turn it on and story would come, filling the air, the page.

Cowley told him, These are too long to sell and
this isn't a novel, as you know. Sit down and write me a
story a day.

He did and he sold three. There were to be two
hundred more.

. . . where he used to live, when he first got here.
633 Hudson Street. Go there. A long walk and what
to do, what to do. And do it.

Smokes, like he would, down Eighth. Traffic all
picante and sharp with metal flashing, moving. Human
voices like streamers curling after sticks, the sun a
steady yellow tone.

Turn down Horatio, shadowed and cool.
Cobblestones like ancient Celtic teeth grayed and
hardened, little latticeworks of light where the rain
has run.

A cold gash of air from a deep garage. Inside,
unattended, a car on a hoist. Beneath it and to the
back a wobbly mirror blinding in southern light.
Walk up to it.

. . . Features in bizarre disproportion, one eye wider
than an ear, the light behind garish, white, without
mercy.

633 Hudson Street gone, now a block of 61 Jane.
The little hovel where he stayed—Walker Evans took a
photo of it—exists only as a photo Walker Evans took
of it.

The imperfect corner below his window can only be stared up from, up at the solid brick of where he used to be, young and thirsty, writing a story a day.

Down Bleecker, over on Christopher, down Waverly to check my mail. No news. Dim projects attracting no light. Stories about the boys, the boy; about the dead father, a guilty one. Old shit.

. . . To the bar, always, inevitably. I don't see him in there, lurking behind the bottles, or within, a winking, cheery eye. No.

A fellow sits down next to me. I know him. I tell him about the writer—a story a day, I say. He says he met him once, in the '60s. Cheever'd suffered a broken leg skiing, and sat in a chair all the while. Still in all, cheerful, he said, and when he discovered it was someone's birthday he led the room in a round of "For He's a Jolly Good Fellow."

Cheerful little man, my friend said again. And very proper. Then those stories, all roaring without mercy, he said. Right then, sunlight flashed in the doorway. Someone came in.

Central Park West

Shakes the pavement, city traffic,
pound of pile drivings and thunder runners,
specter of death rising from the park.

Car tires lick the street,
lifting and replacing
ribbons of rain,

a kind of getting, ripping
and simultaneous healing,
water raised in the treads

and returned, sealed to the roadway
like brand-new cellophane
laying down, keeping

the world fast, secure,
giving the soul some sleep,
the avenue its long, cold face.

Summer Morning

I saw a person get hit in traffic today.
The sound was all the car's
as if the body were just an object
and only the hood could feel: it hollered.

The lump lay still in the street
yielding only silence after.
The queer, spastic angles of the dead,
of tossed or broken dolls, the stillness.

Everyone stopped to listen.
O, for a sound!
Slowly, bystanders began to move
in the thick boxy air, coughing,
clearing throats, making
any kind of noise.

Noise Meter

So open out and hear
the clatter-ticking shoosh of traffic
like the flow of blood
and the buzz of a TV even
on mute, horns,
horns speaking for temperaments
on the street, the guttering gun
of an old car, a jalopy
and the soft swish
of conveyances through rain.

Flesh on flesh—
my hand on my arm,
a high, soft sound
like something being polished
or prepared
in another room.

A two-note *do-don't*
warns a pedestrian
or an encroaching cab.
Hollow voices, subterranean
in the West 4th Street station,
shout down the damp tiled corridors
some overstated drama
that the traffic swallows
and the approaching roar of a train
drains away . . .

My own swallow, the last of the wine,
tendons and the squeak of teeth
on tender tissues loud in my head . . .

The page turns crisply
and the scratch of a pen
is the most desperate sound
and the last, or the highest,
seven stories above the street,
levels more above what matters,
this scrawl in a personal idiom
that could brand me
were I to commit a crime . . .

My wife I can hear, shifting in her sleep.
My boy saws away
in his makeshift tent of a bed.
Cars continue, then a manic address:
He has a gun! Gravely, panicked, and I hear
the beat of soles upon the pavement
and no air, no one breathes, like the night
has been punched, you can hear
breaths suspended, including mine,
the falling away of footfalls
in the moment before a ripping . . .

But nothing. Nothing happens.
A truck roars through its low gears.
Crisis resolves to scurry away.
I don't even get up to see . . .

Just breathe again,
that sound that seems enough then,
then is not enough.

No Answer

It's not all been said.
My kid today: Dad, what's the orange
in fire, is it sun? This boy,
almost five, a sentence never said
in all of history, and me there,
no answer to things, I say
some carbon burning, Son, some ink
in that trash can there, or the paint
from a soda can, maybe wine,
the alcohol burning off, or would that be
blue . . .
                    I recall the blue flaming shots
some other dad threw back
when I was a kid, wondering
what father would drink fire
to have it lick down his chin
like neon, going black before the floor,
and I think I've missed my chance
and that dad's son looked at him
like mine looks at me now, saying,
what next, if fire drips
from fathers' tongues and goes out?

My Quarrel with Language Poetry

I.

Dullsville, as in the after-hours
of a person taken by cancer.
After the alarm.
After the shock.
After the sorrow and the talking
a fact remains:
there is an absence and it is dull.

Survivor and survivors.
Those close, the kin. They
worry about or around
in a candlelight
we don't see in.
It's their smell, their polish;
flowers turn to dust
in their rooms.

Their halls darken.
While ours, now ours
run with children
fighting with the cat,
stumbling over laundry
piles, while I am taking scotch,
goddammit, why not, why not?
And the kids will wake
in the morning.
My kids will wake in the morning.

II.

So my son at six is told
his best friend's father has died.

Told by me and my wife in his bed.
Is this not a fit subject for poetry?

III.

Cancer and quick and what can you say?
He will live with an uncle in New Jersey
and all of his toys. And his father
will join his mother—for now they both have died—

up high in heaven,
and little Jeremy will rise
and be a fine man and will always know
this day as the day things changed
or will he? What will my own boy know
and what will I?

I remember this: my mother in the morning
entering my room, saying to my best friend Jeff,
saying his name, Jeffrey, she says, Jeffrey, waking
him softly, her hand on his shoulder,
Your father passed away during the night,
and if you feel like crying you should just cry,
it's good to cry. And I remember
Jeff's back, we were all of eleven then,
and it didn't shake, he didn't sob.
We lay there for a while
till we smelled blueberry muffins from the kitchen
and we went out and ate them.

—in memoriam, Cary Reich, 1949 – 1998

PART THREE

The Apple

Let's let this run, then,
    like a slide,
a giving over of ourselves
    to a momentum. May-

be in this
    a rhythm will assert itself,
my own praxis
    to emerge and take.

If not everyone's hope,
    at least it's mine,
that these words drop
    into a kind of music

which term we hate
    (to use), knowing what music takes,
and we're so unsure
    of what poems do

and deserve. Even so,
    I've been reading Muldoon,
savant of the half-rhyme,
    and wonder why

he's so inclined
    but not why he's famous.
For there's something some say
    's near organic

about the end of the line, hey!
    and the way it plays
with sound, or the mind's
    expectations, and has since who.

This won't do, of course.
    I can't any more en-
thuse about his sonnets
    than I can about the 'lets'

in a game I don't play
    for I know naught of the names,
and—clerihew!—don't want to.
    The kinds of harms

that befall me
    when I turn to parts
are appalling, so much better
    I seem

in a free form
    on a fallow farm.
The only worm in the apple
    is that it's only an apple.

Still Life: Coney Island & Country Gym

The guys who wrestled
    were French guys mostly—
LaRocques, Drollettes, LaTours—
    tough, farm-hardened boys
from Hardscrabble, across the river.

Certain things must interest you
    and the answers be in language.

Matches were Tuesday and Thursday nights
    in the small, dark gym.
Our grapplers in faded red tights
    with white shorts sewn in
and silly shoes like Superman's.

Five minutes of bliss
    on the beach at Coney Island.

These events were
    sparsely attended.
A few brothers pull up
    in trucks, fathers fresh from mending
duck through doffing feed caps.

Simple: two Heinekens
    stirring in.

I went once, against type.
    Sat by myself in the stands
through ten bouts; then
    it was Jimmy Facteau in the last fight.
He chewed ice all night to make weight.

Waves and old seaside folly.
Clouds of fried food, cerveza fria,
rings of pickled calamari.

He got his face mashed for his efforts,
this bull who'd seldom said a word,
rubbed adub the rubber mat.
When the whistle blew he'd won the match!

On the board-
walk a guy with eyes
like burst blueberries
barks on the phone.
It's noon.

Saranac, too, a victor.
The teammates mob Jimmy Facteau.
There is grace in the dumb gym.
For a second nothing comes in
or out; a moment self-sustained.

"Fuck the calamari!"
"Hey, chief"—to me—
"You got four quarters?"
To the phone, "Don't talk to me markers!"

Equipoise, as a law,
and a raspberry mat burn
on Jimmy Facteau's jaw.
All this holds up the night, turns
beneath it like a cylinder.

My son runs
  across the beach.
I can feel the thrum
  of his feet
through the sand, love.
  I can feel it shaking.

Originally Called "7/20/96"

Days without sentiment
as the occasion for a poem—
beyond judgment, beneath praise,
beyond merriment, without

thoughts of home or love
or musings on love;
without hate, without cause,
without being known.

Unremembered days, blessed and lost.
Twenty thousand breaths ex-
changed with the air
and this to show for it.

❋

But it is my mother's birthday
the (premature) titling tells me;
and twenty-seven years ago
we gassed up at Carter's Texaco,

my father and a carful of kids
bound for Parc Jarry and Montreal,
Mets and Expos, a twin bill,
the Sunday papers all of Chappaquiddick

and my father's troubled brow
as he flipped *The Sunday News*
and the pump rang.

A mess of Little Leaguers
pounded their mitts in the backseat.

❋

My mother was left at home that day
to her backyard and her Coppertone.
Later, on the scoreboard,
word that man had walked the moon.

The Mets lost two that day, I think.
Bob Bailey hit one out,

and Coco Laboy, too, the Expos' *troisième but.*
When we got back that night

the moon hung full and bright,
my mother asleep in her chair.
Her I can call.

❋

As if his face were the moon
and he were asleep
but dead, my boy
lay curled in a yellow bucket

beneath a sink, drowned
in urine, as I fold a newspaper
and tidy up, this dream
of an in-law's bathroom.

And the horror only begins,
is only beginning, for him,
my young son, for me.
And the dreaded imagery

occasioned by nothing
but a dawdling in the afternoon
and the night-leech
of sounds—

Laboy, the sun, the moon,
a mother, death by drowning.
And so we live the news
and relive the news, despite ourselves,

our fathers flipping pages on the hood of a car
as the gas pump dings, dings, dings.

At the Night Game (Flushing, Queens)

Like lyrics from a lost land,
as signs from somewhere else,
words come to hand
and beg our care.

Testimony, in the old sense,
gathers in the air.
You can hear the sounds—
voices, long repaired

to other places, fates
not visible above the ground,
sounding down
to the congregated.

The question "why" suggests itself
but the answer is clear—
love is a distant whisper
and a listening in.

The Death of Robert Creeley

Robert Creeley and I
were driving in a farm truck
on the road above our church
in Redford, New York.

Bob was leathery and dark,
his eye patch gray.
The truck stunk inside like cow meal
and was warm as hay.

The burlap at our feet shuffled
over holes in the floorboard.
Cigarette smoke curled above the dash.

We talked and bockety-wheeled it
along the Priest Road
and then the truck lurched—

through the windscreen Creeley flew.
We jolted
to a stop and Bob slid down the hood past
the bumper. I heard his neck crack, as I was there.

I ran into
an empty house, wide
open to the air
and light
and no one in.
I called a number, thought,
what am I doing
here, I'm going to die

with Robert Creeley and his neck
broke out on the Priest Road. When
I went back

he was
moving his head slowly,
loose on its

stalk, whispering

something about woodwinds.

Or he might have been whistling for me.

February Thaw

Train north . . .

A cabbie gets out of his cab in the breezeway at Penn
Station and slams the door. Steps up on the curb.
Down the front of his pants he puts his hands to the
knuckle and then sweeps each hand round his waistline
till they meet at his back, thereby untucking his shirt.
He then goes back down the front of his pants and
vigorously scratches his balls.

Two women are wrangling with their four children on
the main floor. A boy, ten or so, his face thick with
youth and scared; two little boys like small bears in
identical dark blue toques, about five; and a toddler girl
toddling in a puff of bubble-gum-colored snowsuit.
By the nipple in her mouth and a purple coiling cord
she is attached to her mother's wrist. The mothers
are talking wildly about something. There's the
"All aboard!"

In a track cut through Harlem, a helmet in the snow
like a man buried standing.

A silvered mirror surface sliding whole: ice floes on the
Hudson moving south.

Boats again. The Palisades fall straight in smooth
serration, like a shelf of fudge or a long brick of hash.

Rusted, twisted stairs hang from a trestle out over the
river. Closest to the ice comes a pipe-length of dangling
railing. The stairs end in air.

The ice brash near the shore like a white chenille bedspread.

Obliquity can make you sick. To try it.

A cold embroidery: gulls perch and peck at the edge of where the river's open.

People encamped within their own sounds. A drummer brushes a little silver beneath the acoustic woodwork and the bright-faced vocal. The brushes lend a soft burnish like the polish of a railroad rail.

Indian Point, stylized breasts and penis. The breasts deadly, the penis false.

In grade school Mrs. Whipple, the music teacher, had a wooden stick from which five wires extended along the perpendicular; each wire at its end looped back an inch or so to form a holder into which pieces of chalk were placed. Across the surface of the black-board Mrs. Whipple would run the stick, leaving behind her the five parallel lines of the musical staff. She would then stand the contraption upright in the chalk tray and move her thickly upholstered body back to the left, where she began. With another piece of chalk, her right pinky extended, Mrs. Whipple would make an elaborate G-clef as lovingly as if it were her own initial and she were a little girl admiring it. And then she would announce with a shrill formality: "A G-clef."

Zithering along the trackside, telephone wires swoop
from pole to pole to pole.

Things move in this thaw like an ice-breaker through
the center shipping lane, like that one right there,
moving south on the river. In its wake, shards of
possible argument.

The ice fast again above Rhinecliff, all the way across.

The frozen river as vast as space and just as empty.
Resplendent crust brushed with a diamond varnish,
the shadow of the Rip Van Winkle bridge upon it like
a lonely scribble.

Just south of Hudson (town) it appears a person has
walked out to the middle of the river and walked back.
The snow is broken in drunken arcs from the shore,
some fool saved or discouraged.

Blue Circle Cement barge pushed by tugs. So far,
no northbound river traffic. Only northbound rail.

What look like eskers maybe, long strips of wooded
land shredding the river, where rivers of runoff spilled
eons ago from a receding glacier, leaving in its effluence
gravel and stone. Wasn't this once the Greenland Sea?

A woman sits down in the seat next to me.
"They made the first car a smoking car," by way of
explanation. She opens a ledger. In it, unlined pages
with poems written in her hand. Quatrains.

We're all poets.

Bridge railings of solid steel painted a rubber red,
like the red of rubber crutch tips, of doorstops, of
water bottles. Why? To hide the rust, when it comes?

The Mohawk River, I think, just into Albany, courses
under the train, a solid, sweeping table of snow.

A line of empty side-tracked boxcars hides the sun for
a long moment. Odd colors—orange, lime-green, azure
—coruscating with beards of iron oxidizing but still
perfect in form.

She is scribbling away madly.

I sleep.

We pass Ticonderoga: "The sound that a pencil
makes being sharpened," I tell her. "From Nabokov."
She laughs, and tries it herself: *Ticonderoga, Ticonderoga,
Ticonderoga.*

Staggered shanties for ice fishing on the lake opposite
Port Henry. Dozens of them. She says her father and
his buddies would push an old wrecked car out each
winter and park it by their shacks. Let it plummet
through in the spring. Boys, she says.

Paths through the woods marked by red ribbons.
Criss-crossing tracks of dogs, merry and confused.
It seems they circle round themselves.

Busted wagon angled in a backyard, snow drifted over
its tongue.

A crow stands keen atop a dead tree facing the
southern winter sun.

In the smoking car the maligned, the malignant.
Overweight teenage girls, bra-less and with bad
haircuts, dye jobs, blonde and cinnamon, going to
a dirty brown, hanks lank behind ears misbehaving.
A slow black girl stares up at her fingers working a
braid just between her eyes, crossing them. Ashen men
slumped alone and deeply smoking.

Outside, stands of dead trees leading to the lake.

Two kids working up a huge ball of snow from
their knees wave at the train. The engineer lays on
the whistle.

I tell the woman about the word "brash," for the
choppy jumble of ice near shore. A good word, I say.
In yesterday's *Times,* three words for river ice: fast,
hummocked, brash.

I want to ask her about her eyes—dark brown smudges
beneath them like bruised fruit.

Home . . .

On the swirled frozen cream of Chateaugay Lake,
two long tongues of open water shimmer in a kind of
aluminum ecstasy.

The hills around are inky like sketchings, the spidery
scrawl of trees backlit by snow.

On Chazy Lake, more water running in the sunlight.
A truck drives out on the lake. Will I see it break
through? There are kids in the back. They've stopped.
They are in the middle of the lake. They walk. The two
kids. They run back and forth. The adult is there now,
out of the truck. It is getting warmer. There is another
truck coming across.

In the spring. In the spring the ice thins and cracks and
shifts. The fisherman's jalopy, the woman's father's junk
heap, slowly sinks to its doors. The front end dips down.
The truck and taillights, upright, ease straight in. The
surface closes over it clean.

Water running on a thousand hillsides, dripping with
gentle, pausing caution off the tips of trees. In an
empty snowfield, the soft tinkling of snowmelt in the
inner bank like change.

The melting snow on the surface of the ice starts to
bring the air out of the ice and weakens it.

Train south . . .

From New York to the Vermont side, the water frozen
all the way across.

Loose Mondrian shapes frozen in a Joan Miró space. It
is getting cold again.

The newspaper says: A couple lost on the lake, walking
the mile across. Oh boy. Saturday, too much sun.
Trapped on a floe? A break through the ice? Perhaps
wide pools got them wet, slips and falls, soaked. Night
comes. Now frozen on the pad of ice, or sunk below.

The pace of the thaw is the controlling factor in all
major river systems, someone explains. The gravest
danger is in the valleys, where the rivers slow down
and the gradient is small. The ice breakup can form
dams that divert the flow to surrounding lowlands.
In the higher elevations the power of the water keeps
things moving, someone explains. But the cold air
and the misting water forms frazzle ice, which sticks
to abutments and bridges.

Towns along the rivers can only maintain a riverwatch.
Residents scan the snow drifts between the water and
their homes. At some point, conditions trigger a release
of larvae that have been incubating through the winter.
Tiny winged insects called stone flies emerge from the
bank, traveling toward the sun. Residents know that
the thaw will follow in five to seven days.

The moon like a pale wafer in the afternoon sky. It's
the color of snow. Lake Champlain is a baby baby blue,
like the sky. The train, now, hurtling south.

The setting sun first puts a blush in the eastern sky,
stirring a little blood into the wispy blue; but now
the sky has drained and paled, all but dead for the day.
Night soon, the moon sharpening into a bright
white chip.

The cold, dark iron of Albany, the trestle leading
into the station from the north is the start of a long
sheathed corridor, sharp with evening's deepening
pall and ending in an absolute tunnel underground.
Penn Station.

The search for two people out on the lake has been
suspended. An ice breaker cleared a lane across the lake
today, and the police are using grappling hooks in
hopes of finding the bodies.

Picking Stone

The earth pushing up its stone
in the thaw each spring; the "stone boat"
Gramp's tractor'd pull,
a long iron sheet
at the end of a chain,
up and down the field,
the term is *boustrophedon*
for the path it takes up
the length three rows wide,
a wide turn, and back,
like an ancient form of writing
but picking stone instead.

Behind us, the heads of newborn rocks
finally, after ever, scraped, seeing sun.
And Gramp says "Yup, yup."
We throw them on the boat.

Then we hit a big one.
The linked procession
Whoas to a stop. We get out
the heavy chain, the dented
shovels. We dig down deep
to get the links around
the underbelly (we hope, not the shoulder).
The tractor revs and grinds,
the chain snaps taut,
tightens its bite
as we work in the crowbars
to lever it, like we mean business,
and we heave

to get this boulder up
from God knows where.
"It weren't here last year," Gramp laughs,
knowing that's always the case, two tons
suddenly just there in your potato field
and you pretend surprise.

And here it is, big as some stone mastodon,
black-backed and wet like skin
and wanting to be free, rolled
to the creek and walked on, to feel

the slap of kids' feet
and the water lap, the warm sun,
the dry, brittle wicker of a picnic basket,
the spread of a napkin,
the keening of stars.

Some ambitious stone, this,
but we can't move it.
Darkness fills the field like ore.

"Going nowheres," says Gramp.
"Not this year. Plant around it."

A Dilapidated Foundation
in Clinton County

Just all low broken stones,
no basement dug, from what I can tell.
Limestone, dealt in half-decks
to schist, since the time of Roosevelt.

Ankle-high or so, sharp rocks,
what were the walls,
and all grown up around it
and within, saplings thin and green,
fronds leaning, long dry tongues
like a cat's. You walk hip-deep
in the blurry ferns,
crunch of old glass, murmurs.

It could be a church, this light,
squinting in shafts
through the bower. A hushing
shift, you can feel the pulse
of welcome, as if all this nature
wants you.

And it has you for a moment
in its long blind time, and cannot believe
its luck, something about
what consciousness does
amidst the leaves and the wood
that nature loves. It dances,
turns softly, as if it, too, knows

that "dilapidate" spills from stone.

Touring

I.

Guys who first learned to drive
　　driving tractor, and still

swing wide to make a turn
　　as if pulling a wagon

with their Chevrolets.

II.

Birds falling
　　into the trees

like pepper packets spilled
　　from a line in the sky.

III.

Going places
　　where experience

is not remembered
　　as much as pillaged,

looking for the memory
　　in experience.

IV.

Not fashioned
    like fields

all parceled and planted,
    but a thing which,

going through a rock-cut,
    feels the cold patience

of stone
    and the smell of chill.

V.

Two skid marks
    seem the legs of a man

stopping the heart for a strong second
    with a jolt of fear

braking for panic.

VI.

You pass by
    "Dun Roamin" cabins;

an aggressive sign—"Sirloin Steaks
    Cut to Order"—swings from a porch.

VII.

Looking through a stand
 of trees, the fitful silver

gouting of a hillside stream—
 water still

unburdening the land.

VIII.

Nature
 doesn't tell a story,

it's just a language.
 Signs differentiated

by chance
 and fatedly.

IX.

So why do I
 & why can't I

struggle
 with a broken narrative?
I should hold each end
 each in one hand,

a missing and insufficient link,
 and just jump up and down.

x.

Blessedly, a music stirs
   my gut in time

or an idea does
   and I feel

hungry, not for solid food
   but its opposite,

a nothing in the air.

PART FOUR

Dad's Shoes

He's gone now, and so
poems catch you up with
what you know—the deaths
of fathers, in this case.

But the basement doesn't
know, in this house he built
for twelve grand in 1960.

There his seabag hangs still—
unperturbable canvas
cracked, deflated, coarse,
suspended from a rope
wound somewhere in the war.

Scattered behind the furnace,
beyond burst cartons of books,
a golf shoe and a forlorn
boot, its two rows of eyelets
curling away, spilling
a complexity of laces, yellowed,
untugged for years.

An abandoned bread box in the corner,
black with a peeling floral
decal, sits atop an old
nightstand thickened with
spilled paint and sloshed compounds,
relegated, both, to storing

bolts, nails, hacksaw
blades, crusty bagsful
of fuses, lid-sprung cans
of spackle, sandpaper
sheets curling in their
fierce, tough grades.

It sounds so maudlin—
things aging, old, useless
and unused,
going to rot in the dark
of a cellar thirty-five years old.

And it is. But I see my father
cursing the lace of that boot
on a morning that is my
birthday, and he means
no harm, it's just a lace.

The Saranac River

I look so much better
in the mirror of home
since I left—
a kind of sumac grows at its edges.

Light like a liquid
or a wind streams
over me—a father's word
yields a red berry in the fall.

Their tumbling shapes,
a mother's graces rippling past
burnishing my face—
notions bouldering down the gorge.

I stand in the current
my eyes have opened,
and when they close
the Algonkians walk down from Canada.

I remember
a poem by Theodore Roethke
but vaguely—it is far upstream—
they crushed the red berries for war paint.

Mouthing a torrent of images
a mentor read it to us aloud:
Where the mind can go in poetry, he said.
The river isn't moving, I am.

I'll see them when they come,
dark bent bodies intent in the dawn.
And there's no hurry—
they are chanting the unknown French.

Miles from home like them,
ranked against a warm building,
a poem wades in riverlight,
guessing how a river got its name.

Adirondack Sounds

I put the words in his mouth—
this image of myself,
my son at three years of age.
I say to him

Cadyville, Saranac, Schuyler Falls.
Dannemora, Redford, Beekmantown,
Chazy Lake, pronounced *chez Zee*.
And he says them back to me,

eyes big, his tongue clumsy and sweet,
saying the names of towns of my youth.

I'm far from them now,
these syllables holding mysteries
of places people came to,
of how things were then.

I knew my own—Saranac—
without curiosity.
It was like my name.
But Cadyville was where pretty girls lived,

Schuyler Falls a forest cleared for playing ball,
Dannemora a prison town with tall, tough Irish,
Chazy just a cold, deep lake.

The places are on a map
I never need to study,
just hamlets to drive through.
The people that built them,

the sites there, now gone,
yielded to spells of indifferent offspring,
to places fallen down.
Still, Beekmantown

in my boy's mouth
is a clear parcel of fields
farmed for stone and apples,
Redford the soft fold of our church.

He repeats them to me
as I ask, happy at the drill,
expecting something for his effort.
I give him my confused joy.

I say to him *"Paradise,"*
and hear the pure word.

September

Today on Chazy Lake, a steely gray effluvium spreads
steadily west across the surface, an immensity of
silverine silence.

Today, the afternoon rain clouds blow off; the sun, still
bleary with haze, shines through. You can stare at it for
half a second or more.

Today, I walk on the sloping knoll of a picked cornfield,
my city boots crushing the turned topsoil soundlessly.
Across the valley's run to the river rolls more brown
cornfield, lightly stroked by the poked straw's golden
glow; below, the barns of that farm, then the farmhouse
itself, then just forest down to the road I know but can't
see; forest then to the grassy banks of the Saranac River,
where trout might be nosing to the warmish surface.

As I stand there in the soft furrows, my shadow
two rods long, I hear in the air only four sounds:
a hammer clanging; its after-thud echoing off a barn;
the barking of a distant dog; the whine of a tool held
to a grindstone.

Sitting in the air over the valley there is nothing too
distinct—a pearly something, the radiance of convec-
tion at work, damp becoming vapor through the draw
of the sun, drifting like a curtain to the nudges of a
gentle north wind.

Over the valley it seems a host could be born out of that tossing mist warmed by light, something that would stride down and bless.

Today, parked by the river, my person set upon a rock at the edge of the water's bright barium flow, all seems black and white—light, absence of light; bare, dark, twisted trees on the banks; current swift and serious in its eastward course toward Lake Champlain; black rocks humped in midstream, as if feeding there.

At my feet in the muck, a stiff dance of two six-legged creatures is underway. A hint of color, an orange, a dust of blue; no bigger than a dime, these insects, all leg, the body half a match. They stilt it up the bank, awkward and fast; clenched in mating or in a rape, it is so violent, one working its head inside the other's thorax, digging and twisting, thrusting, then stillness followed by a rapid shudder of wings, like when a propeller finally catches and is a blur—an orgasm, perhaps. Then the wings stop.

I slap the two flies between my note pages to show a fisherman I know.

Shadow Limb

It was a Dr. Murphy
who cut my mother's leg off
below the knee
on December 14th.

It wasn't diabetes, exactly,
but the cumulative effects
of poor circulation, of
not caring to move too much,
of having given up.

I mean of missing Dad.

❋

I signed a "Limb Disposal Agreement,"
allowing the hospital to do
whatever it does
with body parts, even though
there was another option—
assignment to a mortician.

But that seemed too grim.

❋

For an evening, and ever since,
I thought of the 'shadow limb'
amputees are said to imagine,
that sensation of itching or of pain, of
heat, of cold, the dear, unweighted density

of living flesh extended into space
where an arm once was or,
in this case, a lower leg.

I wondered in the waiting room
if Mom would have me scratch it
with a straw, something she'd come to like
in her old days.

She loved Pond's Cold Cream slathered
on the coming-away flesh, and then
a good raking after, nails getting down
to the vasculature, if she could stand it.

But Mom didn't last long enough
to miss the left leg, not long enough to swear
to me, by god,
that it's still there.

❈

Perhaps I *should* have sent
my mother's left leg
to the funeral home
to keep her whole in her grave.

But maybe then I wouldn't hear her voice
or see the shadow of her shoulders
move from room to room,
as if we were in a house we loved,
and the shadows were mine.

New Year's Day

I.

January is a soft, white month,
not as harsh as March, say,
or benumbed like February.

January is snow where I come from,
an ermine coat you wake to one day,
covering every surface like a fact

too beautiful to dispute.
Who would want to shovel it?
And the schools are closed.

II.

Down the hill comes a girl with a horse
on a lead. The horse nods sagely, as if
in agreement with something she's said.

They amble to the road's shoulder
where I stand with my son talking to Uncle Ted.
Ted says his leg is bad.

We stand ankle-deep in the fresh fall
with no threat of cars coming up or down.
It's a holiday in a small town.

III.

Her hair is black, her corduroyed legs stand thin.
She speaks with a local accent touched by college.
I'm renting from Nick Carter up the road,

she says, *and Harley takes the barn.*
He's a Connemara pony. He likes people.
Harley *Yes Ma'am*s with his head.

I look into the horse's dark brown eye.
I see sky, brimmed and round,
and a horseness shying like smoke.

IV.

Oh he's handsome in his lustrous morning coat—
dove-gray, with a sheen like ore sand,
his mane, broom tail, and stockings all jet-black

and he drifts, this gray retinal haze adrift
against the brilliant white
like a blind spot.

Smell his body, face in the shadow of his neck.
Nuzzle the coarse brush—a faint odor
of old rope and barn and distant kerosene.

V.

There is a sifting in the trees.
Limping, Ted takes his leave.
My boy is throwing snowballs in the still air.

Harley flinches once,
then gets used to it, seeing snowballs fly.
On his nether belly she pats him

and chats: *fourteen hands and a runner,* she offers.
Big Harley stamps; his hoof clomps like hollow wood.
From his nostrils twin white plumes.

VI.

He thinks you have some food,
she says to my son. Harley eyes
a snowball being packed.

Gabriel offers it up in his mitten.
Blood-purple horse lips quiver forth and nibble.
Hesitant tongue laps then, steams.

Feet shuffle, mine. The cold comes on.
She vigorously claws at Harley's withers,
and I have my hand on my son, my son.

Adirondacks, Easter Sunday

Experience, in linguistic terms,
is all but shot: the trees
are simply bare, the dead
stand in no relation even
to a distant will. Maybe
it's spirit I'm after and not

the words. The scribble
of the roadside bramble a cold,
soaked soot giving no light.

The lake doesn't shimmer either
in the fading afternoon as much as
shiver, the light fleeing
across its surface like a chill wind.

Where are these things
inherited from, images
of death-in-life in a soul-less vocabulary?
But then you catch the rock cut
at Pokamoonshine, sunwarm sluicing
down the icy face of a god.

❄

Later, to the south, yellow rays and rain.
There's a rainbow coming if the light just holds.

Cassie Pickett's Molasses Cookies

One half-cup sugar,
one teaspoon cinnamon,
half teaspoons ginger, salt. Mix together.

One half-cup shortening,
one egg (not necessary to beat);
half-cup molasses, quarter-cup
cold coffee.

Teaspoon soda,
two cups flour.

Mix all together and bake
at 375 degrees, 12 minutes, as Florence wrote.
Anything with molasses is likely to burn
quicker than without, so I use 350
and watch them.

COLOPHON

This is a first edition copy of *87 North,* poems by Michael Coffey.
Printed in Canada by Hignell Printing, Limited
in a first run printing of 2,500.

Designed and typeset by Kelly Kofron of Coffee House Press.
Adobe Garamond 11.25 / 14
Adobe Woodtype Ornaments 11